THE
RAILROAD
IN AMERICAN HISTORY

THE
RAILROAD
COMES TO
AMERICA
(1820s–1830s)

Karen Bush Gibson

Mitchell Lane
PUBLISHERS
P.O. Box 196
Hockessin, Delaware 19707

THE
RAILROAD
IN AMERICAN HISTORY

The Birth of the Locomotive
The Railroad Comes to America
The Railroad Grows into an Industry
The Railroad and the Civil War
The Railroad Fuels Westward Expansion
Electric Trains and Trolleys

The publisher would like to thank Milton C. Hallberg for acting as a consultant on its *The Railroad in American History* series. He is a professor emeritus of agricultural economics at Pennsylvania State University and has been a visiting professor at universities around the world. His railroad interests began when he attended a railroad telegraphers' school in preparation for a job as a depot agent on the CB&Q Railroad in Illinois. After retiring from teaching, he returned to his railroad interests as a new hobby, during which time he has written about early rail systems.

PUBLISHER'S NOTE:
   The facts on which this book is based have been thoroughly researched. Documentation of such research can be found on page 44. While every possible effort has been made to ensure accuracy, the publisher will not assume liability for damages caused by inaccuracies in the data, and makes no warranty on the accuracy of the information contained herein.

Printing
1   2   3   4   5   6   7   8   9

**Library of Congress
Cataloging-in-Publication Data**
Gibson, Karen Bush.
 The railroad comes to America (1820-1830) / by Karen Gibson.
   p. cm.—(The railroad in American history)
 Includes bibliographical references and index.
 ISBN 978-1-61228-287-9 (library bound)
 1. Railroads—United States—History—19th century—Juvenile literature. I. Title.
 TF23.G49 2013
 385.0973'09034—dc23
                                                2012009423

eBook ISBN: 9781612283616

PLB

CONTENTS

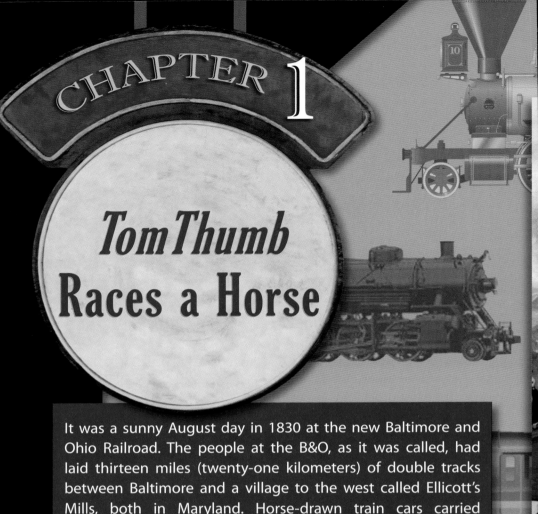

CHAPTER 1

Tom Thumb
Races a Horse

It was a sunny August day in 1830 at the new Baltimore and Ohio Railroad. The people at the B&O, as it was called, had laid thirteen miles (twenty-one kilometers) of double tracks between Baltimore and a village to the west called Ellicott's Mills, both in Maryland. Horse-drawn train cars carried passengers and freight along the tracks that the B&O hoped to extend to the Ohio River, hundreds of miles to the west.

On this day, a new beast of burden—a shiny, black locomotive—sat on one set of rails, belching smoke and puffing steam. It was the *Tom Thumb*, a steam locomotive built by businessman Peter Cooper. Cooper named it *Tom Thumb* because of its small size. Weighing only a ton, it was smaller than British locomotives. However, the *Tom Thumb* would be big enough for Cooper to prove that day that steam locomotives were the future of the railroad.

Peter Cooper was a self-educated man who liked to figure out how things worked. He started as a carriage maker's apprentice before becoming a businessman. He ran a grocery,

The legendary race of the *Tom Thumb* and a horse is a popular story about the beginning of trains in America.

Peter Cooper built the locomotive *Tom Thumb*, in six weeks. He drove the train on its maiden run.

a furniture factory, and a glue factory, where he would later patent a dessert called gelatin.

In 1828, Cooper bought 3,000 acres in Maryland. There was iron ore on the land so he built the Canton Iron Works in Baltimore. He planned to supply the B&O with the iron it used for its rails. Cooper wanted the railroad to succeed.

When Cooper heard about the steam engine being used for trains in Great Britain, he knew this was what the B&O needed. The directors of the B&O had heard rumors that a locomotive wouldn't be able to take the sharp turns planned for their railroad. Cooper was good at inventing things. He told the directors he would build a locomotive that could.

Tom Thumb made the trip to Ellicott's Mills in seventy-two minutes, according to Cooper, who described the ride to the *Boston Herald* two years later.[1] It returned even faster, in fifty-seven minutes. An open-air car attached to the locomotive carried thirty-six passengers—railroad bigwigs and their friends. Accustomed to horse-drawn carriages, they thrilled at the engine's top speed of eighteen miles (twenty-nine kilometers) per hour. Some took out memorandum pads to prove that they could write on a moving train.

Popular stories claim that on the return trip from Ellicott's Mills, the *Tom Thumb* stopped for refueling. The owners of the stage company Stockton and Stokes challenged *Tom Thumb* to a race. They were sure their horses were superior to the newfangled steam locomotive.

A majestic gray horse was harnessed to a car on the tracks next to the *Tom Thumb*. It bolted into the lead. The heavy locomotive was slow to build up speed. Its engine blew clouds of steam through its chimney and made a whistling sound. A rhythm developed between the whistle of steam, rumble of wheels, and hoof beats of the galloping horse.

Both train and horse took the corners with ease. When the engine's blower reached its full power, *Tom Thumb* pulled ahead of the horse. The passengers in the open car shouted for joy.

The *Tom Thumb* was a 1.4-horsepower locomotive. Its vertical boiler was about five feet (one and a half meters) high—and narrower than the kitchen boilers in Baltimore's mansions. Cooper used coal to build a fire in the furnace that heated the water in the boiler until it turned to steam.

A throttle let him open a valve in the boiler to let steam travel into two pipes. Cooper didn't have iron pipes, so he used two rifle barrels that he sawed off himself. They carried steam to the cylinder. The cylinder contained a piston that moved back and forth when steam was pumped into it. The moving piston was connected to rods that turned the locomotive's front wheels.

When *Tom Thumb's* win seemed almost certain with a quarter-mile (0.4-kilometer) lead, a belt came off the blower. The blower caused the fire in the furnace to burn hotter and make more steam to power the piston in the cylinder. Without this draft, the locomotive started to lose power.

A *Tom Thumb* replica

PETER COOPER'S "TOM THUMB" 1829-30 BALTIMORE & OHIO R. R.

Cooper scrambled to replace the belt as the train slowed on the tracks. It was all the horse needed to catch up and race past the *Tom Thumb*. Cooper finally replaced the belt. He tossed more coal in the furnace to build up steam. *Tom Thumb* tried to gain the lead again, but the horse was too far ahead. In the contest of horse versus train, the horse won by a nose.

Many historians claim the fateful race actually took place in September—weeks after the B&O directors took their ride. Either way, the *Tom Thumb* proved that the steam locomotive was a good investment. People rushed to buy bonds in the B&O.

Cheered by its success, the B&O held a contest in 1831 for the best locomotive. The winner of the $4,000 prize was the *York*, designed by watchmaker Phineas Davis. The *York* could pull 15,000 pounds at 30 mph (48 km/h).

The steam engine revolutionized transportation in the still young United States. As they did in Great Britain, trains helped bring the Industrial Revolution to the nation. It would be a time of great and lasting change that opened up the frontiers of the new country. The *Tom Thumb* helped it start.

More than One Tom Thumb

General Tom Thumb and his wife

"Tom Thumb" wasn't just the name for a train. The first mention of Tom Thumb was in a German fairy tale. The Brothers Grimm wrote a version of the fairy tale that became popular. A poor woodsman and his wife wished with all their hearts to have a child. The wife didn't even mind if the child was not much bigger than her thumb.

When the woodsman and his wife received a tiny child, they named him Tom Thumb. Tom Thumb was smart. He helped his parents and others and always outfoxed the bad guys. He was even able to find his way out of the stomachs of both a cow and a wolf! At the end of Tom Thumb's adventures, he found his way home, where he lived happily ever after.

About twelve years after the fateful race of the locomotive *Tom Thumb*, another Tom Thumb appeared in the circus of P. T. Barnum. This Tom Thumb was a man from Connecticut named Charles Sherwood Stratton. He was 32 inches (0.8 meters) tall and weighed 21 pounds. Stratton took on the role of General Tom Thumb in the circus for forty-one years. When he was twenty-four, he married another small person, Lavinia Warren. They took their honeymoon in Washington, D.C. They were entertained at the White House by President Abraham Lincoln and his wife.

CHAPTER 2

The Industrial Revolution Steams to America

Trains might not have been invented if railroads hadn't been invented first. Roads called "wagonways" were used in Germany as early as the 1550s. Wheeled carts with a pin sticking down in the front could ride along on wooden planks. The pin fit into a gap between the planks. This kept the cart's wheels on the wood.

By the 1700s, these roads were becoming common, and more sophisticated. In England, railed roads were good for moving coal, tin, stone, and other heavy loads. On some railways, the cars traveled downhill under their own power, with a brakeman riding onboard. Horses pulled the empty cars back uphill. The goods were usually brought to waterways where they could be shipped to other towns.

Because stiff wheels on a stiff surface meant goods could be moved more easily, people spent a lot of time figuring out the best way to build rails and wheels. By the mid-1700s, some early railways were using strap-iron rails,

Richard Trevithick's
Coalbrookdale engine

In 1802 the Coalbrookdale Compan...
...a steam engine for Richard Tre...
the first railway locomotive in the...

This full scale working replica was...
GKN Sankey in conjunction...
National Vulcan Engineering Insura...
and presented to the Museum on...

Because horses pulled some of the first trains, people used the term "iron horse" as a name for early steam locomotives.

made with thin strips of cast iron fixed onto wooden rails. The wheels on the carts had a flange, meaning they were shaped like an upside-down "L." This let the wheels sit snug on the rails.

Others used plates of cast iron fixed to the wooden rails. In these "plateway" systems, the plate was shaped like an "L" and the wheels did not have flanges.

In the late 1700s, an engineer named Richard Trevithick was working with the steam engines being used in England's mines. The engines powered the pumps that kept the mines from flooding.

Trevithick began building his own high-pressure steam engines. He called his early models "puffers," because of the noise they made. Trevithick decided to put his steam engine on wheels. He knew a locomotive would be more effective than horses at pulling heavy loads.

On February 21, 1804, he made history when his locomotive pulled ten tons of iron on a nine-mile (fourteen-and-a-half-kilometer) stretch of railway between the Penydarren Ironworks and a canal in Wales.

George Stephenson, known as the "Father of the Railways," helped to revolutionize British transportation. Ten years after Trevithick's feat, Stephenson was building practical, reliable locomotives to use on short coal courses. He was a partner in the world's first locomotive company, Robert Stephenson and Company, which opened for business in Newcastle in 1823. It was named after his son, who was a partner in

the business, and who had followed in his father's footsteps and become an engineer.

When a railway was proposed to run between Liverpool and Manchester, Stephenson was hired as the head engineer. In 1829, a competition was held to see which locomotive was best suited for use on the new railway. George Stephenson's *Rocket* won.

Meanwhile, people in the United States were recognizing the importance of a good transportation system. Manufacturers and farmers had a limited market because it cost more to ship their products than what they could make selling them. They needed a way to move their products to more people to help settle the very large nation.

The United States experimented. The sixty-two-mile (hundred-kilometer) Lancaster Turnpike was the country's first long paved road. Opened in 1795, it connected Philadelphia and Lancaster in Pennsylvania.

Early tramways were set up to carry things like coal. They usually led to canals where the coal would be loaded into wooden containers and craned onto boats. The cars were pushed and pulled by men or horses, or by ropes and chains powered by a stationary steam engine.

The first American tramway was completed in 1764 in Lewiston, New York. Two cars were linked by rope over a pulley at the top. When one cart moved down the wooden rails, it pulled the other up. It was used to move bricks, clay, and gravel.

Many of these early rail systems used gravity for the downhill trip. One of the best known was the Mauch Chunk Gravity Railroad in Pennsylvania. In 1820, the Lehigh Coal and Navigation Company finished building a road from its mines on Summit Hill down to its coal chutes in the town of Mauch Chunk (later renamed Jim Thorpe), which sat on the banks of the Lehigh River. The company's first shipment of 365 tons of coal to Philadelphia sold immediately. Miners couldn't dig up coal and send it down the road in horse-drawn wagons fast enough. Not only that, the road could be dangerous and hard to use in bad weather.

The solution was to convert the road to a railroad. Completed in 1827, the nine-mile (fourteen-and-a-half-kilometer) gravity railroad let trains of coal cars—as many as seven hooked together at once—sail downhill on their own. Some of the cars carried the hard-working mules that would get out at the bottom and haul the empty cars back uphill. The tired mules ate on the downhill ride, which took about half an hour. The uphill trip could take as long as four hours.

The railroad eventually became known as the Switchback. It was considered an engineering marvel and second only to Niagara Falls in visitors during the nineteenth century. Soon, people were paying to ride on it. It became the inspiration for American roller coasters.

James Watt of Scotland made vast improvements to the day's steam engines. They required far less fuel, which made them more practical. John Fitch adapted the steam engine to move a ship on the Delaware River in 1787. Steamboats quickly increased on the country's rivers.

The United States began building canals. The Erie, Hudson, and Delaware canals were all important waterways. Canals were useful for moving large amounts of cargo. It might take a team of horses up to a month to move three tons of coal from Pittsburgh to Philadelphia. A steamboat on a canal could haul even more between the two cities in only three and a half days.

The British Way

American engineers began visiting England to study the British railways and their new steam locomotives. In 1825, a group called the Pennsylvania Society for the Promotion of Internal Improvements sent engineer William Strickland to report on the canals and railways of England. The planned Baltimore and Ohio Railroad sent three engineers in 1826. The Delaware and Hudson Canal Company sent civil engineer Horatio Allen in 1828.

Allen's job was to check the new locomotives and see if they would be able to haul coal from mines in northeastern Pennsylvania to Honesdale, Pennsylvania. From there, the coal would travel by canal to

New York City. If Allen thought locomotives could handle the job, he was to buy four, along with sixteen miles (twenty-six kilometers) of iron rails.

Twenty-five-year-old Allen sailed to England, carrying a letter that his former coworker John Jervis wrote for him. It laid out the type of locomotive the company needed. After he arrived, Allen bought one engine from Robert Stephenson and Company. He found the other three in the town of Stourbridge. One of the locomotives was the *Stourbridge Lion*. The lion's head painted on the vertical boiler gave the locomotive its name. The cost of the *Stourbridge Lion* was $2,915.

Allen also purchased 390 tons of iron rails. Each rail was 15.5 feet (4.7 meters) long and 2.5 inches (6.4 centimeters) wide. As the items became available, they were taken to the United States by ship.

The *Stourbridge Lion* arrived in Honesdale in July 1829. It was the first British locomotive to run on American rails. It made its test run on August 8. A crowd showed up to gawk at the giant, hissing hulk of iron.

Many people predicted that railroads weren't practical, including Daniel Webster, a politician known for his speaking skills. He lived in Massachusetts and he believed that the snow

The *Stourbridge Lion*

common in New England winters would cover the rails and make travel dangerous. Newspaper editorials warned that locomotives were the work of the devil. Cartoons in the same newspapers showed trains chasing people through the streets.

People were too scared to climb onto the *Stourbridge Lion*. For that reason, Horatio Allen rode alone. He also had to operate the train, something he had never done before.

When the *Lion* started moving, the nervous crowd's mood quickly changed to one of excitement. They cheered as Allen rode over a wooden trestle bridge and across the Lackawaxen River.

Allen said that "when the cheers of the onlookers died out as I left them on the memorable trip, the only sound to greet my ears until my safe return, in addition to that of the exhaust steam, was that of the creaking of the timber structure."[1]

As Allen and the locomotive disappeared from sight, people wondered if he would return. Within minutes, the *Lion* roared back into sight. The locomotive was running backward with a happy Allen at the throttle.

The engine performed well, but it ran on a track designed to support four tons. The *Stourbridge Lion* weighed at least seven and a half tons—far more than what Jervis had called for in the specifications he wrote out for Allen. It was too heavy for the strap-iron and soft hemlock rails of the Delaware and Hudson Canal Company's tracks. They quickly lost their shape under its weight. The *Lion* was retired not long after its maiden run.

John Stevens: "Father of the American Railroad"

John Stevens III was born in 1749 in New York to successful parents. They owned a lot of land and a fleet of ships on the Atlantic Ocean. After attending King's College (now Columbia University) in New York City, Stevens joined the Patriot Party. The American Revolution was about to begin. At twenty-seven, Stevens became a captain in George Washington's army. He was later promoted to colonel. For the rest of his life, people called him Colonel Stevens or Colonel John.

John Stevens

After the war, Stevens started a steamboat business. In the early 1800s, his company built most of the steamboats in New York waters.

However, Stevens came to believe that steam-powered railroads—not canals—were the future of the nation. In 1812, he published a pamphlet titled *Documents Tending to Prove the Superior Advantages of Rail-Ways and Steam Carriages Over Canal Navigation.* His pamphlet was called "the birth certificate of all railroads in the United States."[2]

Stevens persuaded the legislature that New Jersey should invest in a railroad. In 1815, lawmakers agreed. The New Jersey Railroad Company was granted the first railroad charter in the United States. The railroad, which would have linked Trenton and New Brunswick, wasn't built because no one wanted to invest the great sums of money it would take.

The biggest supporter of the Erie Canal, a politician named DeWitt Clinton, sent the Colonel a letter challenging him to prove that steam railroads could work. By then Stevens was seventy-six, but he took up the challenge, building what he called a "steam wagon." The wagon ran on a 660-foot (201-meter) circular track on his estate in Hoboken, New Jersey, puttering along at 12 mph (19 km/h). It was most likely the first steam locomotive built and run in America.

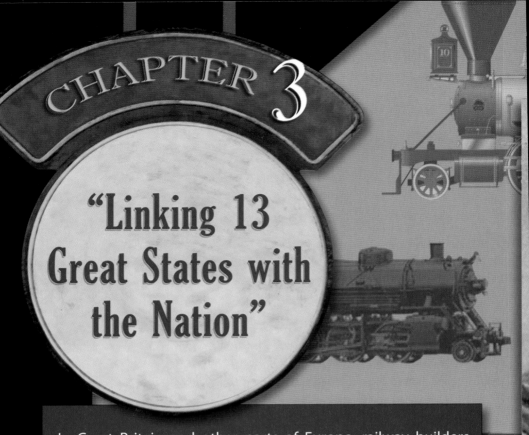

CHAPTER 3

"Linking 13 Great States with the Nation"

In Great Britain and other parts of Europe, railway builders tried to keep their tracks as level and straight as possible. This was especially important in the early days of locomotives when they still weren't strong enough to haul heavy loads up steep hills and they couldn't make sharp turns. The British spent lots of money cutting into the land and building huge embankments, bridges, and long tunnels. It could take hundreds of workers years to complete some of these massive projects.

But in America, tracks had to go long distances, make sharp curves, and snake around or over hills and mountains. They were the first roads to many places in the new country. Engineers and other people working on the railroad had to find new ways to make the grade as they did things for the first time.

The Leiper Railroad in Pennsylvania was the first American railroad to be surveyed. An 1809 map laid out the plan for

The railway stations of Great Britain were known as railroad stations or depots in America. Stations bustled with activity in the early nineteenth century as both passengers and freight were loaded and unloaded.

tracks connecting Thomas Leiper's quarry and stone mill on Crum Creek to his landing on Ridley Creek. The wooden tracks ran for three quarters of a mile (1.2 kilometers). Horses pulled single cars with flanged iron wheels along the track.

The Granite Railway in Massachusetts was another early railroad, and the first chartered railroad to eventually become a common carrier, meaning it would haul passengers and freight for whoever was willing to pay. Gridley Bryant was only thirty-six when he designed it. He had already lived a lifetime of hard work. His father died when Bryant was young. Bryant knew he had to support his family. At fifteen, he was apprenticed to a Boston builder. Apprenticing was a way for young men to learn a useful skill and support their families. When he learned all that he could from the builder, Bryant started his own business.

On March 4, 1826, Bryant and a partner incorporated the Granite Railway Company. Construction began in April, and the railroad opened in October. It cost $50,000 to build and only $10 a year to maintain. Wooden rails topped with thin iron plates were placed on stone crossties atop a bed of crushed granite. The wooden-and-iron rails wore out fast, and they were replaced with stone rails that were also capped with iron. Eventually, rails made entirely of iron were laid. The track's gauge, the distance between the two rails, was five feet (one and a half meters).

The Granite Railway had its test run on a Saturday. Sixteen tons of granite was loaded onto three cars. A single horse pulled the attached cars from the Bunker Hill Quarry to the Neponset River nearly three miles (five kilometers) away.

Bryant introduced new ideas for the young railroad industry, such as the portable derrick, the switch, and the turntable. The derrick loaded cargo into the train cars. The switch allowed the train to change to another set of tracks. The turntable was a big, spinning platform that could turn a train car around to travel in the opposite direction.

Bryant also employed an eight-wheeled car, which was useful for carrying loads of granite that averaged six tons. It helped spread the

heavy load so the tracks wouldn't wear out as fast. Bryant's car had huge wheels that stood six and a half feet tall. The cars carried their granite loads under the axles.

The granite was loaded onto a platform between the tracks. Then the car was rolled over it. Chains were attached to the platform. The loaded platform was raised a little above the track by machinery at the top of the car.

Bryant didn't patent any of his ideas. He thought they should benefit everyone.

In 1830, a new section of the railway was added. Train cars moved up the 315-foot (96-meter) incline on a cable. Two years later, the Granite Railway had one of the first fatal railroad accidents in the United States. Four men were riding on the upward trip when the cable snapped. It sent the railway car over a cliff. One man was killed and the other three were seriously hurt.

Birth of the B&O

The Baltimore and Ohio Railroad is often called the nation's first common carrier railroad (although some give that credit to the Granite Railway, since it was formed first, but didn't become a common carrier until later). The B&O wasn't designed to move specific cargo from a mine, quarry, or mill. Its trains carried passengers and hauled freight for anyone with money to buy a ticket or pay the haulage. The railroad's directors started service with horse-drawn cars, but they eventually hoped to use steam locomotion. They were carefully watching Great Britain's progress. When the B&O's first tracks were laid, they used the British gauge of 4 feet 8.5 inches (1.4 meters).

The "Ohio" in the Baltimore and Ohio Railroad's name referred to the Ohio River, not the state. The plan for the B&O was a 380-mile (612-kilometer) railroad that would travel from Baltimore to a town called Wheeling on the banks of the Ohio River. At that time Wheeling was in Virginia. It later became part of West Virginia, which broke away from Virginia in 1863 during the Civil War.

Going beyond the Ohio River was a big deal in the early 1800s. Everything beyond the river was considered the West. The railroad would have to go through the rough and rugged Allegheny Mountains on its way to Wheeling.

The B&O received its charter on April 24, 1827, and construction began the following year. A Maryland businessman named Charles Carroll was one of the directors of the B&O. He attended the railroad's groundbreaking ceremony on July 4, 1828. The cornerstone that was laid that day still exists. At ninety-one, Carroll was the last living signer of the Declaration of Independence. As he dug the first shovel of earth he told the people gathered that day, "I consider this among the most important acts of my life, second only to my signing the Declaration of Independence, if even it be second to that."[1]

The Delaware and Hudson Canal Company received its charter a year earlier than the B&O, but the B&O started construction first. Baltimore was desperate to avoid financial disaster. Canals from other major ports threatened to make Baltimore and its harbor unnecessary. The Erie Canal, completed in 1825, opened up shipping between New York City and the Great Lakes. Digging began in 1828 on the Chesapeake and Ohio Canal, which would connect Washington, D.C., with Cumberland, Maryland. In Pennsylvania, the Main Line of Public Works was building a system of canals and railroads to link Philadelphia and Pittsburgh.

First the B&O built the thirteen miles of track where the *Tom Thumb* steamed along on its maiden voyage. Within five years, 135 miles (217 kilometers) of track had been laid.

The B&O reached Washington, D.C., by 1835. It began carrying U.S. mail in 1838. By 1842, the B&O connected to Cumberland, Maryland. Ten years later, it finally reached Wheeling. The B&O's motto became "Linking 13 Great States with the Nation" as it continued to grow. It lasted for 160 years, before being absorbed by another transportation company on April 30, 1987.

Like other early railroads, the B&O started with cars pulled by horses. It also experimented with cars that had a horse run on a treadmill inside the train. The first train to use this type of actual horsepower was called the *Flying Dutchman*. It traveled thirteen miles (twenty-one kilometers) in ninety minutes.

The railroad also tried wind power by building a car with a sail. Wind power raised the speed of the train to fourteen miles (twenty-three kilometers) per hour. However, wind wasn't reliable and unless it

The *Flying Dutchman*

was blowing in the right direction, the car was useless. The B&O's chief engineer called the sail car "a clever toy."[2]

After the *Tom Thumb* showed what it could do, railroad owners and engineers knew that horses, inside or in front of the train, and sails weren't practical for long distances or trips across steep mountains. The answer lay in steam power, and by July 1831 all of the B&O's trains were using it.

The South Carolina Canal and Railroad Company, started by local merchants, had set down 136 miles (219 kilometers) of track by 1833 to become the world's longest steam railroad yet. It connected the South Carolina cities of Charleston and Hamburg. The rails were laid on a series of wooden piles that made it easier to span swamps and uneven ground without as much digging. As with much of the backbreaking labor in the South at that time, slaves did a good portion of the work.[3]

Canals gave railroads competition, and some railroads were abandoned. Others merged. The Mohawk and Hudson Railroad and the Saratoga Railroad, both in New York, and the Boston and Providence Railroad in Massachusetts joined the B&O.

The first railroad stations were often in hotels, old houses, or even lean-tos. In the 1830s, the Mount Clare station in Baltimore became the first train depot. It was built on a hilly parcel studded with hickory trees—land donated to the B&O by James Carroll, a distant relative of Charles Carroll. It was the place to buy tickets and send or pick up packages. Station agents were in charge of the early depots.

Eventually, the federal government took on a greater role, such as providing surveys for state-owned railroads. The Philadelphia and Columbia Railroad was the first state-built railroad. It was part of the Main Line of Public Works project that used rails and canals to link Philadelphia with Pittsburgh. By this time, steam engines had opened up train travel for both cargo and passengers.

Horsepower

James Watt

If you have an interest in cars, motorcycles, or boats, you probably already know about horsepower, or HP. Even the power of lawnmowers is measured in HP. Before steam, diesel, hydraulic, and electric engines, horses often provided the power to move things, and that included moving cars along railroads. It was with steam engines that the term "horsepower" was first used.

When James Watt revolutionized the steam engine, he compared it to the power of a horse. He figured that a horse could lift 33,000 pounds at a speed of one foot per minute. This was one unit of horsepower. The equation was 33,000 foot–pounds per minute, or 550 foot-pounds per second. A foot-pound is a unit of work or energy. (One foot-pound is equivalent to 1.35 joules.)

Watt and others used this information to show the public how much more powerful trains were than horses. The first trains could produce the same amount of energy as a dozen workhorses. An added benefit was that since trains weren't living things, they didn't need to rest.

Soon, manufacturers were using horsepower, shortened to HP, to measure the power in anything that moved, from electric gardening tools to racing cars. Even the horsepower of humans can be measured. The average horsepower of a person is 0.1 HP. Athletes, particularly runners, have a faster HP.

James Watt contributed another measurement to society—the watt is named after him. We see that measurement used most often with lightbulbs, where a watt is the current multiplied by the voltage.

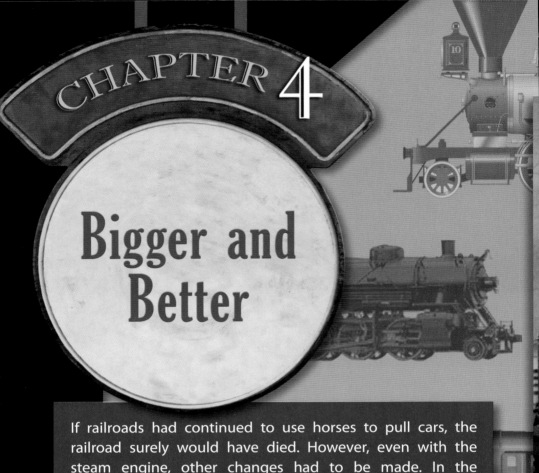

CHAPTER 4

Bigger and Better

If railroads had continued to use horses to pull cars, the railroad surely would have died. However, even with the steam engine, other changes had to be made. In the beginning, the United States still looked to Great Britain for new ideas for railroads.

By 1829, British engineer George Stephenson had made important improvements in the steam locomotive. One of those was a small steam-brake cylinder for the brake shoes on the locomotive. The steam brakes were safer than the previous cable brakes.

Strap-iron rails didn't last long under the heavy weight of the locomotives. Tracks improved when the rails were made completely of cast iron. By 1821, a British iron works produced even stronger wrought iron rails, also recommended by Stephenson.

By 1830, Americans were opening their own ironworks to produce rails. Blast furnaces created a crude type of iron

The parts for the *John Bull* were shipped from Great Britain in1831. Mechanic Isaac Dripps put it together without an instruction manual.

called pig iron. The pig iron was melted in a furnace to create wrought iron. Wrought iron could be pressed into shape before it cooled.

Changes were made to train wheels, too. James Wright saved wear on the flanges and reduced resistance by inventing the cone-shaped wheel in 1829. Unlike flat wheels, the cone-shaped wheels let a train shift slightly on the tracks so that it could round corners more easily. Trains had fixed axles, so it was a problem for them to go around curves where the outside wheels needed to travel farther than the inside wheels. Cone-shaped wheels let the entire axle slide to the side, so that the fatter part of the cone rode on the outside rail of the curve, and the thinner part rode on the inside rail.

In 1831, Robert Stevens, a son of Colonel John Stevens, went train shopping in England. He shipped back parts for the *John Bull* for the Camden and Amboy Railroad in New Jersey. He asked a mechanic, twenty-one-year-old Isaac Dripps, to put the steam locomotive together.

Dripps had never seen a steam locomotive and had no instructions for putting one together. Not only did he assemble the locomotive, he also made improvements. British railroad tracks were straight, while American ones were not. The *John Bull* kept running off the tracks until Dripps loosened the front wheels. He also added a bell, headlight, and a cowcatcher. The cowcatcher was a V-shaped wedge on the front of the locomotive that pushed aside any objects that might derail the train, including cows that sometimes wandered onto the tracks.

The *John Bull* ran regularly for thirty-five years. Once retired, it still appeared at state fairs and expositions. It became the property of the Smithsonian Institution in 1884. In the 1970s, people wondered if the *John Bull* could run one more time, perhaps on the 150th anniversary of its first trip. On September 15, 1981, the *John Bull* thrilled crowds once again at the Old Georgetown branch in Washington, D.C.

The South Carolina Canal and Railroad Company hired a new chief engineer, Horatio Allen, the same man who drove the *Stourbridge Lion* on its first trip. Allen convinced his employer that it was time to move from horse-drawn cars to steam locomotives. He told the company's directors, "There is no reason to expect any material improvement in the breed of horses in the future while, in my judgment, the man is not living who knows what the breed of locomotive is to place at [our] command."[1]

Allen's employer bought an American-built steam locomotive from the West Point Foundry in New York. The West Point Foundry was one of the first American companies to build locomotives. The locomotive was named the *Best Friend of Charleston*. Weighing four and a half tons, the locomotive's steam engine created a pressure of fifty pounds per square inch (50 psi).

The *Best Friend of Charleston* took its first trip on Christmas Day in 1830 with 141 passengers. A brass band played and fireworks lit the sky. According to the *Charleston Courier,* the locomotive "flew on the

A replica of the
Best Friend

wings of wind at the speed of fifteen to twenty-five miles per hour, annihilating time and space . . . leaving all the world behind." [2]

The *Best Friend of Charleston* worked well for a year. Then the boiler blew up. The person in charge of the fire that heated the water to make steam was called a fireman. The fireman of the *Best Friend of Charleston* had grown tired of the sound of escaping steam and tied down the safety valve. Pressure built up and the boiler exploded, killing the fireman, scalding the engineer, and destroying the *Best Friend*.

Lighter and Faster

With the success of the West Point Foundry, other inventors and engineers experimented with building locomotives. One thing Americans tried was building lighter engines. The first American locomotives weighed half as much as their British counterparts. Even at a lighter weight, the *DeWitt Clinton* was able to pull five railroad cars

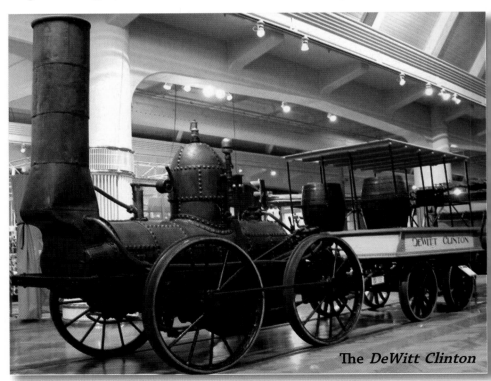

The *DeWitt Clinton*

between Albany and Schenectady at up to twenty-five miles (forty kilometers) per hour. Railroads and canals were sometimes bitter rivals. Despite that, the *DeWitt Clinton* was named in honor of the New York politician who was responsible for getting the Erie Canal built, and who exchanged letters with Colonel Stevens about which mode of transportation was superior. Clinton died in 1828 while he was governor of New York.

The *DeWitt Clinton* was the first steam engine on the Mohawk and Hudson Railroad in New York in 1831. The locomotive lasted two years. The *South Carolina* was another locomotive that went into service in 1831. It was an eight-wheeled engine at a time when most had four wheels.

The Mohawk and Hudson Railroad had been smart enough to hire John Jervis away from the Delaware and Hudson Canal Company. In 1832, the skillful engineer built them the *Brother Jonathan*, a locomotive with a four-wheel leading truck in front of its driving wheels, which were the wheels that got power from the engine. This leading truck helped support the locomotive, and because it was attached in a way that let it swivel independently, it helped guide the locomotive around curves. The new technology allowed the *Brother Jonathan* to reach the incredible speed of sixty miles (ninety-seven kilometers) per hour.

The early twentieth century would introduce the Whyte notation, a way to classify locomotives by using three numbers to describe their wheel arrangements. It was devised by Frederick Whyte and counted the number of leading wheels, driving wheels, and trailing wheels. British locomotives often had trailing wheels, but most American locomotives did not.

Jervis was the first engineer to design a 4-2-0 locomotive, and it was called the "Jervis type" in his honor. Locomotives like the *Brother Jonathan* had a four-wheel leading truck that guided it around curves and two powered driving wheels on a rear axle beneath the locomotive's firebox. It didn't have trailing wheels.

The *Atlantic* showed great improvements in speed, power, and cost when placed on the B&O railroad in 1832.

In 1832, the B&O placed the *Atlantic* on the tracks. The vertical-boiler locomotive hauled 50 tons for 40 miles (64 kilometers), running at 15 mph (24 km/h). The *Atlantic* did the work of forty-two horses for half the cost. Unlike British trains that burned bituminous coal, the *Atlantic* burned hotter, cleaner anthracite coal mined in eastern Pennsylvania.

The *Atlantic* was nicknamed "Grasshopper" by workers because of its drive mechanism. The engine had a horizontal beam and long vertical rods that looked like insect legs when they were in motion.

Although many American railroads were using the same gauge as British railways, their trains were becoming taller, longer, and faster as the 1830s unfolded. Frontiersman Davy Crockett commented, "I can

only judge of the speed by putting my head out to spit, which I did, and overtook it so quick that it hit me smack in the face."[3]

With so many people inventing things for the railroads, arguments broke out over who owned the new technology. In 1834, Ross Winans received a patent for an eight-wheeled railroad car to use on the B&O. Winans sued the New York and Erie Railroad when they began using an eight-wheeled car.

The case lasted five years and went all the way to the U.S. Supreme Court. It was ruled that Gridley Bryant had invented the eight-wheeled car, and Winans had simply improved it. No one ended up benefitting financially from the invention. In fact, Gridley Bryant died penniless.

Taking a Ride

The first American passenger train cars looked like open stage coaches pulled by horses. By the 1830s, passenger cars were enclosed and had a center aisle with seats and windows on either side. These were different from the private, comfortable compartments of the British.

The American cars had hard seats that gave a bone-jarring ride. Stoves at the end of each car were supposed to warm the passengers, but there wasn't any way to move the heat. On winter days, most passengers were still miserably cold.

Open train windows on hot summer days allowed smoke from the engine to pour into the cars. Fiery ashes burned holes in people's clothing.

Nighttime rides were pitch black except for a couple of candles in each car. Children made a living for their families by selling hot bricks in winter to warm people's feet or their food and drink. It wasn't until after 1840 that the railroads began to provide more comfort for their passengers.

Sometimes the rides contained surprises. Writer Samuel Parker was traveling from Ithaca, New York, to New York City in 1837 on the Mohawk and Hudson Railroad. At one point, he and the other male passengers had to jump off and help push the train when it stalled on

The first passenger trains had cars that looked like stagecoaches. People dressed up for the experience of riding on a train.

a curve. During a stop at Little Falls, the conductor heard a rumor that a bridge farther down the line was going to be blown up by "the Erie Canal men, who fought the cars because they damaged the canal interests."[4] Passengers had to wait while the bridge was inspected. No explosives were found and the train crossed safely.

Matthias Baldwin

Old Ironsides

Matthias Baldwin was born on November 10, 1795, in Elizabethtown, New Jersey. He was apprenticed to a jewelry maker. He later worked as a printer and an engraver. Baldwin was first known for improving the process of printing calico, which is cotton cloth with a pattern on one side. He also created his own steam engine to provide power for his shop.

In 1831, the Philadelphia Museum asked Baldwin to build a model of a four-wheeled locomotive. It was so well done that the people at the Philadelphia, Germantown, and Norristown Railroad hired him to build a full-sized locomotive to replace their horse-drawn cars. Baldwin built *Old Ironsides*. It could pull 30 tons and run at 28 mph (45 km/h).

Old Ironsides was such a success that the Baldwin Locomotive Works of Philadelphia soon opened for business. Baldwin's second locomotive used a steam engine with very high pressure—120 psi. This American locomotive was more powerful than British locomotives. During Baldwin's lifetime, his company built more than 1,500 locomotives.

In addition to being a key person in America's Industrial Revolution, Baldwin fought against slavery and supported the right to vote for African-American men. Baldwin was such a strong abolitionist that the South refused to use his locomotives during the Civil War. Matthias Baldwin was inducted into the Inventor's Hall of Fame in 2005.

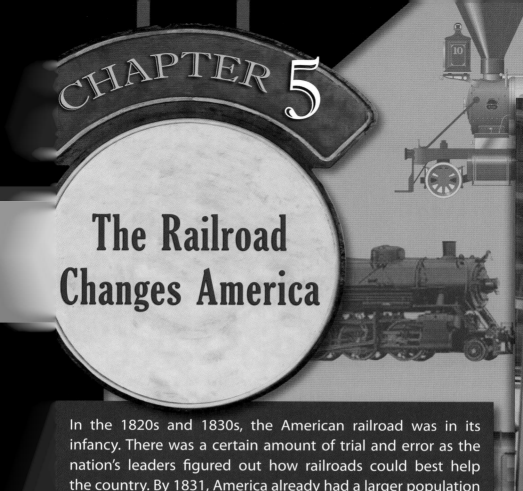

CHAPTER 5

The Railroad Changes America

In the 1820s and 1830s, the American railroad was in its infancy. There was a certain amount of trial and error as the nation's leaders figured out how railroads could best help the country. By 1831, America already had a larger population than Great Britain and a lot more room to grow.

The railroad changed the world, but nowhere was that change as huge as it was in the United States. The writer Ralph Waldo Emerson called the railroad "a magician's rod, in its power to evoke the sleeping energies of land and water."[1] Railroad fever spread throughout the United States. In 1837, hundreds of projects were planned as railroads spread to new states like Kentucky, Ohio, Indiana, and Illinois.

Many early railroads ran alongside rivers and canals. Other railroads worked as partners by transporting goods to the canals for shipping. Canals usually cost less to use than railroads, but they didn't go everywhere. Furthermore, the top speed for boats on canals like the Erie was only four miles (six and a half kilometers) an hour. Trains were reaching

The *Lafayette,* named after a Revolutionary War hero, was one of the first steam locomotives built with a leading truck.

speeds five times faster. This was better for shipping perishable crops like fruits and vegetables.

In 1832, the B&O charged businessmen about a quarter of what they paid to ship the same goods along turnpikes. Boston businessmen figured that shipping by railroad cost them one-third of the amount to move products in horse-drawn wagons. The costs of shipping by railroad continued to drop. From 1815 to right before the Civil War, the cost of moving goods by train dropped by 84 percent.

Shipping by train wasn't just cheaper, it was faster. The 200-mile (322-kilometer) journey between Boston and Albany once took several days of hard travel. Trains reduced the trip to a few hours. It once took a day for a trip between America's two largest cities, New York and Philadelphia. Although only 90 miles (145 kilometers) apart, the trip required two boat rides and a stagecoach ride. By the 1830s, it was a short train ride.

Rail transportation not only provided a way to move people and goods from one place to another, it opened up new lifestyle opportunities for Americans. People no longer had to remain close to each other and to towns. Trains allowed people with wanderlust to pick up and move. They opened up the West for settlement. Great cities like Chicago were created on the backs of the railroads. Agriculture grew rapidly as trains moved products to the market in an affordable and timely way.

More change was coming. Canadian railroads like the St. Andrews and Quebec Railway began operating in the 1830s and would soon connect with U.S. railroads across the border. The first telegraph wire would also be strung along the B&O.

The *Reuben Wells* was a helper train designed to push other trains up the steepest tracks in the United States in the mid-1800s.

Locomotives steamed into America in the 1820s and well before the end of the century, they would become instrumental in the nation's westward expansion.

Businessmen like Asa Whitney looked even farther. What if there was a railroad to the West? He asked Washington, D.C., to think about the trade possibilities. Easy access to America's West Coast would make trading with China much easier.

The locomotive and railroad may have been borrowed from England, but the United States had made them bigger and better. By the end of the 1830s, more than 3,000 miles (4,800 kilometers) of track had been laid in the eastern United States. This was more than all of the track in Europe. In America, it was just the beginning.

Monopoly

Darrow Monopoly
set, 1933

Charles Darrow of Pennsylvania played a game of buying and trading property in the early 1930s. Without a job during the Great Depression, Darrow spent time creating his own version of the game. He introduced it in 1933 and sold it for $4. Within a year, he couldn't keep up with the demand. He sold the rights to Parker Brothers and retired as a millionaire. The game was Monopoly, one of the most well-known games in the world. More than 275 million Monopoly games have been sold.

B&O. Reading. Pennsylvania. Short Line. To any board game fan, these are easily recognized as the four railroads ringing the board of the seventy-five-year-old game.

The B&O Railroad was the Baltimore and Ohio Railroad, one of America's first railroads. The Reading (pronounced "Redding") Railroad began as the Philadelphia and Reading Railway when it started in 1833. By the late nineteenth century, it was just the Reading Railroad. The Pennsylvania Railroad, called "the Pennsy," was based in Philadelphia. At one time it was one of largest railroads in the world. It merged with New York Central Railroad in 1968. All three railroads closed in the 1970s and 1980s. Only the Short Line wasn't a specific railroad, but rather what short-distance railroads were called.

1774 James Watt makes important improvements to the steam engine. The Industrial Revolution begins.

1804 Richard Trevithick builds a steam locomotive for a Welsh railroad.

1809 A survey map is made for the Leiper Railroad. It is the earliest known American survey map for a railroad. The tracks are laid down the following year.

1815 The first American railroad charter is granted to the New Jersey Railroad Company.

1823 George Stephenson opens the world's first locomotive workshop in Newcastle, England.

1825 Colonel John Stevens builds a "steam wagon" that he runs on a level circular track at his estate in Hoboken, New Jersey.

1826 The Granite Railway is built and opens in Quincy, Massachusetts. Its owner, Gridley Bryant, invents exciting new technology.

1827 The Mauch Chunk Gravity Railroad is built in Pennsylvania.

1826 The Delaware and Hudson Canal Company is granted a charter to build a railroad.

1827 The Baltimore and Ohio Railroad is granted a charter for a railroad from Baltimore to the Ohio River in what is then Wheeling, Virginia.

1829 The *Stourbridge Lion* is the first steam locomotive to run on the tracks of the Delaware and Hudson Canal Company. James Wright invents the coned wheel, which prevents wear of the flanges and makes it easier for locomotives to take curves.

1829 James Wright invents the coned wheel, which prevents wear of flanges and makes it easier for locomotives to take curves.

1830 The Camden and Amboy Railroad is chartered in New Jersey. Peter Cooper builds the *Tom Thumb* and tests it for the Baltimore and Ohio Railroad. The *Best Friend of Charleston* is built at the West Point Foundry in New York for the South Carolina Canal and Railroad Company. It is the first completely American-built steam engine to go into regular service. It is also the first American train to provide regular passenger service.

1831 The *DeWitt Clinton* becomes the first steam locomotive on the Mohawk and Hudson Railroad. Robert Stevens goes to England and buys the parts for the *John Bull* for the Camden and Amboy Railroad in New Jersey, and mechanic Isaac Dripps then puts it together, even though he has never seen a locomotive.

1832 The *Brother Jonathan* is built by John Jervis for the Mohawk and Hudson Railroad. It is the first locomotive with a four-wheel leading truck. *Old Ironsides* is built by Matthias Baldwin for the Philadelphia, Germantown, and Norristown Railroad.

1833 George Stephenson invents a steam-brake cylinder to operate brake shoes on the driving wheels of locomotives.

Chapter 1. *Tom Thumb* Races a Horse

1. William Sloane Kennedy, *Wonders and Curiosities of the Railway* (Chicago: S. C. Griggs and Company, 1884), pp. 42–43, http://www.todayinsci.com/C/Cooper_Peter/CooperPeter-TomThumb.htm

Chapter 2. The Industrial Revolution Steams to America

1. Oliver Jensen, *The American Heritage History of Railroads in America* (New York: American Heritage Publishing Co., Inc., 1975), p. 26.
2. James Alexander Jr., "John Stevens: The Man and the Machine," Railroad Museum of Pennsylvania, http://www.rrmuseumpa.org/membership/milepost/stevens.pdf

Chapter 3. "Linking 13 Great States with the Nation"

1. Christian Wolmar, *Blood, Iron, & Gold: How the Railroads Transformed the World* (New York: Public Affairs, 2010), p. 13.
2. William H. Brown, *The History of the First Locomotive in America* (New York: D. Appleton and Company, 1874), p. 110, http://johnwood1946.wordpress.com/2011/09/14/the-earliest-american-railroads-and-steam-locomotives/
3. Henry Schultz and His Town of Hamburg, SC: "The South Carolina Canal and Rail Road Company," http://arete-designs.com/shultz/scrr/

Chapter 4. Bigger and Better

1. Aaron E. Klein, *Encyclopedia of North American Railroads* (New York: Exeter Books, 1985), pp. 13–14.
2. The Best Friend of Charleston Railway Museum: "History," http://bestfriendofcharleston.org/
3. Oliver Jensen, *The American Heritage History of Railroads in America* (New York: American Heritage Publishing Co., Inc., 1975), p. 32.
4. Ibid, p. 22.

Chapter 5. The Railroad Changes America

1. James P. Ronda, "America's Frontier Forever Changed," *American Heritage,* Volume 58, Issue 4, Spring/Summer 2008, http://www.americanheritage.com/content/america's-frontier-forever-changed

"The American Railroads: A Long and Storied History." American-Rails. com. http://www.american-rails.com/

Del Vecchio, Mike. *Railroads Across America: A Celebration of 150 Years of Railroading*. Ann Arbor, MI: Lowe & B. Hould Publishers.

Douglas, George H. *All Aboard! The Railroad in American Life*. New York: Smithmark Publishers, 1996.

"History of Railroads and Maps." The Library of Congress, American Memory. http://memory.loc.gov/ammem/gmdhtml/rrhtml/rrintro.html

Jensen, Oliver. *The American Heritage History of Railroads in America*. New York: American Heritage Publishing Company, 1975.

Klein, Aaron E. *Encyclopedia of North American Railroads*. New York: Exeter Books, 1987.

Martin, Albro. *Railroads Triumphant: The Growth, Rejection, and Rebirth of a Vital American Force*. New York: Oxford University Press, 1992.

Museum of the American Railroad: The Trains that Built Our Nation. http://www.museumoftheamericanrailroad.org/

Pacey, Arnold. *Technology in World Civilization*. Cambridge, MA: The MIT Press, 1991.

"Railroad History." Pacific Southwest Railway Museum. http://www.sdrm.org/history/timeline/

Wolmar, Christian. *Blood, Iron, and Gold: How the Railroads Transformed the World*. New York: PublicAffairs, 2010.

York, Thomas. *North America's Great Railroads*. New York: Dorset Press, 1987.

FURTHER READING

Books

Coiley, John. *Train (DK Eyewitness Books)*. New York: Dorling Kindersley Publishing, 2009.

Isaacs, Sally Senzell. *Stagecoaches and Railroads (All About America)*. New York: Kingfisher Books, 2012.

Isaacs, Sally Senzell. *The First Railroads (The American Adventure)*. Chicago: Heinemann-Raintree Classroom, 2004.

O'Mara, Jack. *How Railroads Shaped America,* New York: Rosen Classroom, 2009.

Runte, Alfred. *Trains of Discovery: Railroads and the Legacy of Our National Parks.* Lanham, MD: Roberts Rinehart Publishers, 2011.

On the Internet
B&O Railroad Museum
    http://www.borail.org/
B&O RR Photo Tours
    http://www.trainweb.org/oldmainline/
Best Friend of Charleston
    http://bestfriendofcharleston.org/
National Postal Museum: Moving the Mail
    http://www.postalmuseum.si.edu/exhibits/2c_moving.html
Social Studies for Kids: History of the Railroad
    http://www.socialstudiesforkids.com/subjects/railroadhistory.htm

GLOSSARY

abolitionist (ab-uh-LISH-uh-nist)—Someone working to stop slavery.

axle (AK-suhl)—A rod in the center of a wheel. On a train, each pair of wheels is connected by a straight axle, and called a wheel set.

boiler (BOI-lur)—A tank that heats water.

bond—A certificate issued by a government or a public company promising to repay borrowed money at a fixed rate of interest at a specified time.

canal (kuh-NAL)—A channel dug across land in order to connect two bodies of water

cargo (KAR-goh)—Freight that is carried by train, ship, or aircraft.

charter (CHAR-tur)—A formal document that states the duties of a group.

current (KUR-uhnt)—A flow of electricity..

cylinder (SIL-uhn-dur)—In a steam engine, a tube-shaped chamber that contains a piston.

depot (DEE-poh)—A railroad station.

derrick (DER-ik)—In a train, a tall object with a long, moveable arm that can raise or lower heavy objects.

diesel (DEE-zuhl)—A fuel used in engines that is heavier than gasoline.

engineer (en-juh-NEER)—A person who designs and builds engines, machines, or public works. On a train, the engineer is the driver.

exposition (ek-spo-ZISH-uhn)—A large exhibition.

ferry (FER-ee)—A boat that carries people across a stretch of water.

fleet (FLEET)—A group of ships, cars, or airplanes.

gravity (GRAV-uh-tee)—The force that pulls things down.

hydraulic (hye-DRAW-lik)—Operated by liquid moving in a tight space under pressure.

inducted (in-DUK-ted)—The process of admitting someone into a special group.

legislature (LEJ-iss-lay-chur)—A group of people with the power to make or change laws.

locomotive (loh-kuh-MOH-tiv)—An engine used to pull railroad cars.

mechanism (MEK-uh-niz-uhm—A system of moving parts in a machine.

Morse code (MORS code)—A code where letters are represented by combinations of long and short signals of sound or light.

patent (PAT-uhnt)—A legal document that gives an inventor the sole rights to make or sell the invention.

perishable (PER-ish-uh-buhl)—Likely to spoil quickly

quarry (KWOR-ee)—A place where stone or rock is dug from the ground.

sheath (SHEETH)—A close-fitting cover.

steam (STEEM)—The vapor that forms when water boils

surveyed (SUR-vayd)—Studied in order to make a map.

switch—A mechanical device that is used on a track to switch a train to another track

swivel (SWIV-uhl)—To turn or rotate on the spot.

telegraph (TEL-uh-graf)—A system for sending messages over wire.

throttle (THRA-tuhl)—In a steam locomotive, a handle used by the engineer to open and close a valve controlling the steam flow from the boiler to the cylinder, which contains a moving piston.

trestle (TRESS-uhl)—A framework that supports a bridge or railroad track.

voltage (VOHL-tij)—The force of an electrical current.

wrought iron (RAWT eye-uhrn)—A processed form of iron that is easy to shape but is strong.

ABOUT THE AUTHOR

Karen Bush Gibson is the author or more than thirty educational books about various places, cultures, historical events, and people. She enjoys taking photographs of old trains and historical train depots. She also loves riding on trains!